Michael and Jane Pelusey

THE MEDIA

Newspapers

MACMILLAN
LIBRARY

First published in 2005 by
MACMILLAN EDUCATION AUSTRALIA PTY LTD
627 Chapel Street, South Yarra 3141

Visit our website at www.macmillan.com.au

Associated companies and representatives throughout the world.

National Library of Australia
Cataloguing-in-Publication data

Pelusey, Michael.
Newspapers.

Includes index.
For upper primary school students.
ISBN 0 7329 9291 5.

1. Newspapers – Juvenile literature. I. Pelusey, Jane. II.
Title. (Series: Pelusey, Michael. Media).

070

Edited by Anne Löhnberg and Angelique Campbell-Muir
Text and cover design by Ivan Finnegan, iF Design
All photographs and images used in design © Pelusey Photography.
Cover photograph: Reading a financial newspaper, courtesy of Pelusey Photography.

Printed in China

Acknowledgements
Michael and Jane Pelusey would like to thank the Royal Western Australian Historical Society (Inc.),
The *Sunday Times* and the Community Newspaper Group for their assistance.
The publisher is grateful to the following for permission to reproduce copyright material:

All photographs courtesy of Pelusey Photography.

While every care has been taken to trace and acknowledge copyright, the publisher tenders their
apologies for any accidental infringement where copyright has proved untraceable. Where the
attempt has been unsuccessful, the publisher welcomes information that would redress the
situation.

Please note
At the time of printing, the Internet addresses appearing in this book were correct. Owing to the
dynamic nature of the Internet, however, we cannot guarantee that all these addresses will remain
correct.

CONTENTS

When a word is printed in bold, you can look up its meaning in the glossary on page 31.

THE MEDIA

People communicate in many different ways. One thing common to all forms of communication is that a message is conveyed. Communicating is about spreading information and sharing it with others, in spoken and written words as well as in pictures.

The different means we use to communicate are called media. Each of them is designed to spread information and news, entertain people or let them share experiences. The audience can be one person or a million. Forms of communication that reach millions of people at the same time are called mass media. They include:

◎   newspapers
◎   film and television
◎   the Internet
◎   magazines
◎   photography
◎   radio.

The media have great influence in our everyday lives. They inform us about current events, expose us to advertising and entertain us.

Media play an important role in a family's life.

4

NEWSPAPERS

Newspapers are a popular printed medium. The pages contain news articles, opinion pieces and general-interest stories. Newspapers are published daily, weekly or monthly.

Newspapers are made up of sheets of paper that are printed on both sides and folded in half. A large newspaper is usually called a broadsheet, while a newspaper half that size is called a tabloid.

Reading a tabloid (left) and a broadsheet (right)

The cost of newspapers is kept low. Sometimes newspapers are offered free of charge, to attract more readers. Most newspaper publishers make money by selling advertising space on the pages. Companies promote their products or services in the advertisements.

Number of readers

A major city or national newspaper often has a big **circulation** and is read by hundreds of thousands of people. Newspapers in small country towns may have a circulation of a few hundred or less. Newspapers with a larger circulation are usually more popular with advertisers, as they reach more people.

Customers in Honduras read the news while their shoes are being shined.

EARLY NEWSPAPERS

Newspapers were the first form of mass-media communication. Historians think newsletters and printed brochures about noteworthy events began to appear in Europe in the 1300s. The first regularly published newspaper started in Germany in 1609.

The *London Gazette* (originally called the *Oxford Gazette*), published in 1665, is considered the first British newspaper. In 1704, the *Boston News-letter* became the first continuously published newspaper in the United States of America. Around that same time, the first daily newspaper was published in the United Kingdom.

Growing numbers

For many years, newspapers were published in limited numbers, because most people could not read. Also, the old printing techniques could only produce a small number of newspapers at a time.

Old newspapers

In 1812, a German engineer called Friedrich Konig developed a steam-driven printing press. This huge machine could print large numbers of newspapers at a much lower price. From then on, many new newspapers were printed. It was the beginning of the mass media's influence on people throughout the world.

Improved printing

Until the 1960s, newspapers were printed using the hot-metal method. It was a messy procedure. After complicated preparations, molten metal was poured over plates on which the words were arranged in the right order. This resulted in a mould that the printing machine used to print pages on paper.

Today, printing presses use plates that have been exposed to a negative image of the page. **Typesetters** do not set individual letters anymore. All the information that goes into a newspaper is sent to computers at the printer.

A modern newspaper office

Computer advances

Computers now play a vital part in all stages of newspaper production. They are used to write articles, make changes to photographs and lay out the pages. Since the development of the Internet, journalists can e-mail their stories instantly from anywhere in the world.

The changes that have made newspaper production more efficient, have also brought more competition from other media. The news now reaches the public faster on television, the radio and the Internet than it does in the daily newspaper.

A negative film is used to produce printing plates.

TYPES OF NEWSPAPERS

There are several different types of newspapers. They differ in how often they are published and in their style.

Daily newspapers

Major daily newspapers publish information about news and events in big areas such as a city, a state, a country or the world. A new **edition** of the daily newspaper is produced every day of the week, except on Sunday, when a special Sunday newspaper is produced.

All over the world, people read newspapers as they travel to work.

Daily newspapers usually come out in time for people to read them on the bus or train on their way to work. They tell people what has happened the day before or overnight. Some daily newspapers come out in the afternoon.

Weekly newspapers

Some newspapers are only printed once a week. They contain fewer news stories, because these stories are already covered in the daily newspapers. To make up for a lack of current news, weekly newspapers concentrate on longer **feature** stories.

NEWS FLASH

FAMOUS NEWSPAPERS OF THE WORLD

The *New York Times* (USA)
The *Washington Post* (USA)
The *Times* (United Kingdom)
The *Daily Telegraph* (United Kingdom)
The *Sydney Morning Herald* (Australia)
The *Age* (Australia)
Le *Monde* (France)
The *Times of India* (India)
The *New Zealand Herald* (New Zealand)

Newspapers around the world

Sunday newspapers

Most people enjoy having Sunday off from work or school. It allows them to relax while reading the newspaper in bed, over breakfast or during the day. For this reason, Sunday newspapers usually include longer feature articles as well as light entertainment sections. Important news stories that have been reported in daily newspapers during the week are covered in more depth in the Sunday newspaper.

Community newspapers cover local events, such as this street festival.

Community newspapers

Events that happen in small towns, suburbs and country communities are not usually covered in the major newspapers. Smaller community newspapers cover the news and other issues that are important to local regions, such as town planning issues.

Special-interest newspapers

Some newspapers specialise in just one topic, such as sport, music or finance and business. The articles are aimed at people who are especially interested in that subject.

NEWS FLASH

FAMOUS SPECIAL-INTEREST NEWSPAPERS
The *Wall Street Journal* (finance)
The *Financial Times* (finance)
British Soccer Week (sport)
Sporting Life (sport)
New Musical Express (music)

Businessmen often read more than one financial newspaper.

9

WORKING ON NEWSPAPERS

Every newspaper has many people working together to produce the final product.

The editor

The editor has the overall responsibility for what goes into each edition of the newspaper. Editors make decisions about the main story and the **headlines.** They determine the contents of the newspaper and choose pictures to illustrate articles. Most editors also write a column, giving their personal opinion on a current topic. This is called the editorial.

The editor at work in his office

Sub-editors

Sub-editors are responsible for the **layout** of the newspaper. They use special computer programs to make sure articles, photographs and advertising fit on each page of the newspaper. Other sub-editors read all the articles, **edit** them and make sure the grammar and spelling are correct. They also add headlines and photograph **captions**.

Journalists

A journalist does an interview over the phone.

Journalists write the articles for the newspaper. They research a story and interview people about the topic they are writing about. Sometimes a journalist specialises in one subject, such as travel, politics or sport. Some journalists write their articles from home and sell them to different newspapers for publication. They are called **freelance** journalists.

Photographers

Photographers take photos to illustrate some of the articles in the newspaper. Today's newspaper photographers tend to use **digital** cameras, so they can e-mail or transfer their photographs straight to the editor's computer.

Newspaper photographers are skilled at taking photographs that catch the attention of the reader. They can be employed by the newspaper or work on a freelance basis.

A photographer takes a photograph of an environmental group.

Advertising staff

The people in the advertising department sell space in the newspaper to businesses wishing to promote their products or services. The price of an advertisement depends on its size and on the position in the newspaper.

The people in the advertising department sell advertising space in the newspaper.

Graphic designers

Graphic designers are people with special artistic computer skills. They design advertisements and feature pages so they catch the eye of the newspaper readers. Graphic designers often use computers to manipulate photographs.

A graphic designer creates an advertisement.

FROM IDEA TO NEWSPAPER

Every newspaper begins with many ideas for articles. This is the first stage in creating a newspaper. After the ideas have been developed, there are several other important stages before the newspaper is complete. The stages on the flow chart show how all types of newspapers are created.

Stage

1
IDEAS AND PLANNING

The newspaper staff make plans for the next edition of the newspaper at an editorial meeting. They discuss current events and work out ideas for stories. Each subject is then given to a journalist.

Stage

2
RESEARCH AND INTERVIEWS

Journalists arrange to interview people who are involved in the story. Interviews are done by telephone or face-to-face. The journalists asks questions to find out relevant information for the articles.

Stage

3
PHOTOGRAPHS

Photographers are given stories for which they need to take photos. The style of each story determines which kind of photographs are needed. Sometimes the editor or journalist selects photos from their archives.

Newspaper case studies

Read the six stages from idea to newspaper on pages 14–23 for three different newspaper case studies:

CASE STUDY 1
A Sunday newspaper front page

CASE STUDY 2
A travel feature

CASE STUDY 3
A community newspaper

The busy printing room

Stage

WRITING

The journalists write their stories or articles on computer. Each article must be clear and easy for the readers to understand. How much space is available for each story depends on how important that story is.

Stage

EDITING AND LAYOUT

Sub-editors take the finished articles and check they are the right length, and that the grammar and spelling are correct. They place the articles, photographs and advertisements on each page of the newspaper.

Stage

PRINTING

The finished layout of the newspaper is sent to the printer by computer. The newspapers are then printed, folded and put together.

Upcoming stories are discussed during the daily or weekly editorial meeting and news items are allocated to journalists and photographers. Ideas can come from **press releases**, the Internet or from investigations by journalists after contact with the public. Journalists who specialise in areas such as politics or sport inform the editor about possible stories that could be of interest to the readers.

Stage

1

CASE STUDY 1

A SUNDAY NEWSPAPER FRONT PAGE

John, the editor of a Sunday newspaper, meets with his staff to decide what the most important issues are. He then gives one or more subjects to each journalist. John asks Nadia, a journalist, to write a story for the front page. It is about a royal wedding. He decides the article will take up half the front page and include one photograph.

John, the editor, meets with the journalists one by one.

1

CASE STUDY 2

A TRAVEL FREATURE

The travel editor of a daily newspaper has received a letter from a freelance journalist. It describes his idea for an article on cycling in the Australian outback. Because the travel editor likes the idea, he contacts the freelance journalist, telling him to go ahead and write the article. It will fit in well with a five-page section the newspaper is planning on travelling in the Australian outback.

The article will be about an outback cycling trip.

1

CASE STUDY 3

A COMMUNITY NEWSPAPER

Editors receive many press releases every day, via e-mail and fax, from government departments, organisations and businesses. They include announcements and detailed information about upcoming events.

The editor of a community newspaper has received a press release from the local government on art and local culture. The editor decides to run a story related to this information, because it affects the people who read the community newspaper.

A press release arrives via the fax machine.

2 RESEARCH AND INTERVIEWS

Research involves finding out as much as possible about a topic. Information can come from books, magazines, other newspapers and the Internet, and also from talking directly to people who are involved in the issue.

Talking to people for research is known as interviewing. The journalist prepares some questions to ask, then listens carefully during the interview to understand the issue. This may also lead to further questions. The journalists takes notes during the interview or records the conversation.

Nadia uses the Internet to do research for her story.

CASE STUDY 1

A SUNDAY NEWSPAPER FRONT PAGE

Nadia, the journalist, researches the details of the story for the front page. The story involves an international event, and Nadia finds most of the information using the Internet. There are many sources of information on the Internet, and they need to be double-checked to make sure they are correct.

CASE STUDY 2

A TRAVEL FEATURE

Ross, the freelance journalist, went on a trip with a cycling tour guide last year. Now that he knows the editor is interested in the article, Ross pulls together all the information he has about the cycling adventure. He contacts the tour guide for up-to-date information on the costs and dates, and asks if anything has changed since he did it. Ross interviews other people who went on the trip, so he can include their opinions and **quotes** in the article.

Ross interviews the tour guide over the phone.

CASE STUDY 3

A COMMUNITY NEWSPAPER

The journalist, Stuart, reads the press release and then tries to find out more information. One way he does this is by contacting the department that sent the press release. Stuart also talks to people in the local community, to make the article more interesting. He asks questions to find out their opinions.

Stuart interviews a local artist about his interest in the art grant.

3 PHOTOGRAPHS

Photographs are used in newspapers to give a story more visual impact or to highlight the people who are involved. They add interest to the newspaper and may attract people to read the articles on that page.

Stage 3

CASE STUDY 1

A SUNDAY NEWSPAPER FRONT PAGE

The photograph on the front page must capture the attention of people buying the newspaper. As the front-page story is from another country, the photograph used is sourced from an international agency that sells photographs.

Stage 3

CASE STUDY 2

A TRAVEL FEATURE

Ross checks through the photographs he took on last year's cycling trip. He selects a range of pictures to send to the editor. The editor will pick photos that fit the page and best illustrate the story.

Checking the photographs from the cycling trip

Stage 3

CASE STUDY 3

A COMMUNITY NEWSPAPER

Media press releases are often sent to newspapers with photographs that can be used with an article. Sarah, the editor, decides whether they are suitable to use with the story. She chooses one, and the others are kept on file for future use.

Three photographers are sent with the press release to the newspaper.

The writing that goes into a newspaper is very important. Journalists use a computer to write their articles. They must be careful to make sure their facts are correct, as well as spelling and grammar. Articles usually have a structure made up of an introduction, the body of the article and a conclusion.

Stage 4 — CASE STUDY 1

A SUNDAY NEWSPAPER FRONT PAGE

Nadia puts togeher her information. She writes her article, keeping in mind how much room is available on the front page.

Nadia writes the front-page article on her computer.

Stage 4 — CASE STUDY 2

A TRAVEL FEATURE

Ross writes a 1000-word article about his experiences cycling in the Australian outback, as requested by the editor. He includes a fact file with information about the cost of tours, what they include and details so readers can find out more information from the cycling tour company.

Stage 4 — CASE STUDY 3

A COMMUNITY NEWSPAPER

Stuart writes the article, using information from the press release and from the research and interviews he has done. To make sure the article has an original style, Stuart does not copy the press release word for word. Stuart checks which photograph has been chosen by the editor for the article.

Stuart uses information from the media release to write his article.

5 EDITING AND LAYOUT

Today's newspaper technology allows layout and editing to be done on computers by a group of sub-editors. These computers are linked in a network within the newspaper company. Special computer programs are used to make the layout of each page of the newspaper simple. Each article, photograph and advertisement is placed on the page, then **proofread** for spelling errors, article length and grammar.

Stage

CASE STUDY 1

A SUNDAY NEWSPAPER FRONT PAGE

A team of sub-editors receives the the finished article about the royal wedding from Nadia. The layout sub-editor, Steve, places it on the front page and makes room for a headline. He also places the photograph on the page. Another sub-editor edits the article down to the right size. He also reads the article carefully, checking its spelling and grammar. He writes a headline to catch people's attention.

The sub-editor, Steve, lays out the front page.

The travel editor selects slides for the cycling article.

Stage
5

CASE STUDY 2

A TRAVEL FEATURE

Ross, the freelancer, e-mails the finished article to the travel editor, Alan. Alan reads the article and edits it to fit in the space. He writes a headline to match the article. Then he looks at the photographs Ross has sent in and chooses the ones that best illustrate the article. Advertising space is sold for the travel features to make sure those pages pay for themselves. Most of the advertisements have some relation to the travel industry.

Stage
5

CASE STUDY 3

A COMMUNITY NEWSPAPER

The editor reads the article Stuart has written and edits it. The article and photograph are e-mailed to the sub-editors so they can lay it out and fit it into the allocated space. They also add a headline. All the articles, photographs and advertising need to be edited and the whole newspaper is finished to go to the printer by the **deadline**.

Sub-editors do the layout of the community newspaper.

21

Stage

6 PRINTING

Each newspaper is printed on a huge machine called a printing press. A roll of paper weighing 1300 kilograms unrolls and passes through the printing press to make newspapers. The machinery is mostly automatic, but printers oversee the entire operation. They make sure the colours are correct and lined up exactly, and that the machines fold the newspaper neatly.

Stage

6

CASE STUDY 1

A SUNDAY NEWSPAPER FRONT PAGE

When the newspaper is finished, it is sent to the printer. A photographic negative of each page is transferred onto an aluminium plate, which is placed in the printing press. Rollers apply ink to the plate, where it only sticks to the areas with words or images. Water prevents the ink from spreading all over. This is called the offset process. The ink image is applied from the plate to the paper. Then the pages are cut to size and folded in order. Finally, the newspapers are ready to be sent out on trucks.

Robots move the huge paper rolls around.

The full-colour inserts are ready to be put in the newspapers.

CASE STUDY 2

A TRAVEL FEATURE

The travel section comes as an **insert** in the newspaper. The insert is printed before the regular newspaper. The travel section is inserted automatically by machines after the rest of the newspaper has been printed. Sometimes people are hired to place smaller brochures into the newspaper by hand.

CASE STUDY 3

A COMMUNITY NEWSPAPER

Many printing companies print several different newspapers to make money. To fit in with other newspaper printing times, the community newspaper has its own printing time allocated to it. Since community-style newspapers cover local areas, they do not have the big print numbers or runs of the daily newspapers. Some newspapers are so small they need to do their own printing and do not share facilities with others.

The printers use machines to check the print quality.

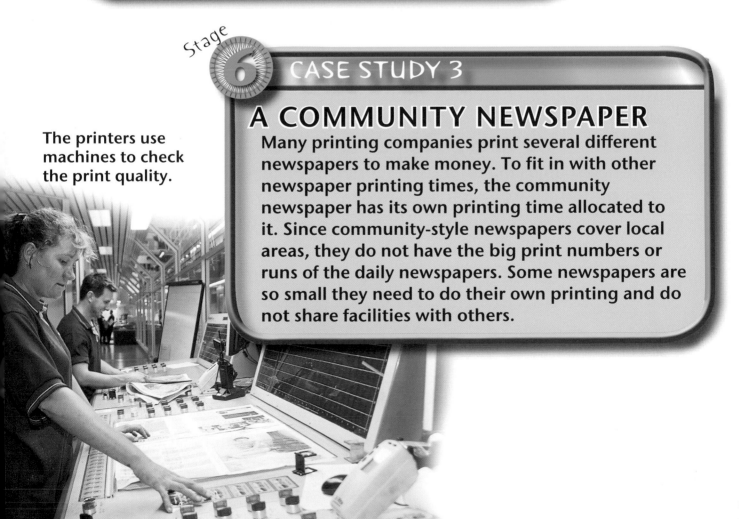

DELIVERING THE MESSAGE

Once the newspaper is printed, it can be **distributed** to the public in a variety of ways. Most daily newspapers have more than one edition printed in a day.

The first **print run** of a daily morning newspaper is sold on the streets late at night. Stacks of newspapers are also loaded onto trucks and planes to be transported to country regions. If a major event occurs overnight or during the morning, the next print run can be altered to accommodate these changes.

Billboards entice customers to buy the newspaper.

Newspaper sellers

Newspapers are sold to the public at shops called newsagencies and at news stands. A range of newspapers arrives every morning to be sold to the public. Newspaper headlines are often placed on **billboards** to catch the attention of buyers.

Free newspapers

Some newspapers make all their money from advertising. They are handed out at train stations or delivered free to people's homes. Many community newspapers are offered to the public in this way. Newspaper companies hire people to deliver the newspapers to household letterboxes. The delivery of newspapers by this method is called a newspaper round.

The community newspaper is delivered to household letterboxes.

Subscription

Many people prefer to have the daily newspaper delivered to their home. They pay monthly or even once a year for a **subscription**. A subscription is usually cheaper than buying the newspaper every day. After the newspapers have been printed, they are rolled up and sent out to be delivered. In city suburbs, newspapers are often delivered by being thrown out of a car and they land in people's front gardens. They are usually covered with clear plastic, so they do not get wet in the rain or under garden sprinklers.

Some newspapers are wrapped in plastic for delivery.

Reading a newspaper on line

The Internet

Many newspaper companies offer **on-line** versions of their newspapers on the Internet. These are available to everyone who has a computer with an Internet connection in their home or workplace. Since the Internet is worldwide, people can access newspapers from other countries. For access to some articles you may be required to pay.

25

CAREERS IN NEWSPAPERS

Newspapers are an interesting field to work in. People who work for newspapers have done university courses or gained their experience in practice.

John is an editor

"I started out as a **cadet** journalist. During this time, I studied journalism at university while working at a newspaper. I worked my way up through the system in the newspaper industry. Now I am an editor."

John is the editor of a Sunday newspaper.

Wayne is a sub-editor

"I started in the newspaper industry as a trainee journalist. We learned on the job as cadets. Eventually I worked my way through the system to became a sub-editor."

Wayne works as a layout sub-editor.

Lindsay is a photographer

"I studied journalism at university and did photography as an extra subject. I liked taking photographs, so I covered a sporting event and took the photos to a community newspaper. They liked the detailed captions and photographs, so they gave me a job."

Lindsay likes working as a photographer.

Nadia is a journalist

"I studied journalism at university. The course taught me research, writing and how the media work. I have worked for several newspapers since I left university. In this job you meet interesting people and you learn something new every day."

Nadia likes the variety of working as a journalist.

Susan works in the advertising department

"I have had years of experience in sales in other areas. I applied for a job at the newspaper after seeing an advertisement. I like my work, and the people I work with are great."

Susan calls people up from the newspaper office.

Greg scans photos for a newspaper

"I originally did an apprenticeship as a compositor. This started my interest in graphics and layout. Compositors are no longer needed in the newspaper industry. I still work in graphics and layout, but everything is now done on computers. When they brought in the new negative film plates, I learned how to operate the equipment on the job."

Greg uses the computer to adjust an image he has scanned.

NEWSPAPERS IN SOCIETY

Newspapers play an important role in our society. They report the news in more depth than radio or television programs. Members of the public can express their point of view in a letter to the editor, appearing on a special page in the newspaper.

Freedom of the press

Freedom of the press is considered very important in democratic countries. In the early years of newspaper publishing, articles that were critical of government decisions were often **censored**. Then laws were developed to change this. It is vital that journalists can write freely when they are investigating political and other important issues, without fear of being arrested or mistreated.

The freedom of the press might be under threat as more and more media outlets are owned by a few big organisations. Big newspaper and media owners (called media moguls) are powerful, wealthy people. Newspapers are careful not to be biased politically or be influenced by their owners.

Sorting through the letters to the editor

NEWS FLASH

MEDIA OWNERSHIP
Rupert Murdoch developed News Limited, one of the world's largest media companies. He started working in media by inheriting an afternoon newspaper in Adelaide (South Australia).

Some people own many television networks, magazines and newspapers.

Entertainment

Reading newspapers can be entertaining as well as educational. Features cover a wide range of popular subjects, such as fashion, motoring, travel and sport. Readers can explore their next holiday destination or read about a car they are interested in buying. Newspapers also tell us what events are happening in our region, such as movies, concerts and sporting events.

Old and new cars are a subject covered in the motoring section of the newspaper.

Advertising

Selling advertising space to big companies is a major source of income for newspapers. If a newspaper publishes a story that is critical about a particular company, that company may not want to advertise in it anymore. Some people fear that big companies, paying many thousands of dollars for advertising space, may influence which stories get printed.

Celebrity news

People all over the world love reading about celebrities, movie stars and pop stars. Newspapers sell more copies if they contain details about famous people's private lives. Some newspapers and magazines have special journalists and photographers who keep track of what celebrities are doing. They are called paparazzi.

Celebrity photographers

THE FUTURE OF NEWSPAPERS

When radio and television were developed in the 1950s, newspapers lost some of their importance in society. Technology continues to reduce the influence of newspapers in our time.

News is available on the radio and television more quickly than in the newspaper. The Internet gives people up-to-date news instantaneously. For that reason, many newspapers have an on-line version, with staff constantly updating the news.

The sales of newspapers have gone down in the 2000s. Newspaper managers look for ways to encourage readers to buy their newspaper, such as competitions and special liftout magazines. Some newspaper owners are buying other forms of media so they can still make a profit.

Future technological developments will probably bring more drastic changes in the newspaper industry. However, some things never change. Newspapers continue to be popular on weekends, when many people have time for a relaxing read.

NEWS FLASH

NEWSPAPERS ON THE INTERNET
The *New York Times*
www.nytimes.com
The *Guardian*
www.guardian.co.uk
The *Australian*
www.theaustralian.news.com.au
The *New Zealand Herald*
www.nzherald.co.nz
The *Japan Times*
www.japantimes.co.jp
Le *Monde* (in French)
www.lemonde.fr

Would you rather read an on-line version or a paper copy of the newspaper?

GLOSSARY

billboards	large advertising posters
cadet	a trainee or apprentice
captions	descriptions that go with pictures
censored	when parts of a story are removed so the public does not read them
circulation	the number of newspapers that are sold
deadline	the time by which something must be completed
digital	using a computer signal
distributed	made available to people in different places
edit	to revise and correct a text
edition	one printing of a newspaper issue
feature	an in-depth article
freelance	not working for one company
headlines	titles of articles
insert	an extra section that is put into the main newspaper
layout	the design of a newspaper page
on-line	available over the Internet
press releases	announcements sent to journalists to inform them about events or subjects, sometimes called media releases
print run	a batch of the same newspapers from a printing press
proofread	when a text is checked, looking for mistakes
quotes	the exact words said by people who have been interviewed
subscription	an arrangement where the reader pays to have the newspaper delivered regularly
typesetters	people who place the text on the page for printing

INDEX